# Collins
# ROMANS

## FASCINATING FACTS

Published by Collins
An imprint of HarperCollins Publishers
Westerhill Road
Bishopbriggs
Glasgow G64 2QT
www.harpercollins.co.uk

First published 2016

A catalogue record for this book is available from the British Library

ISBN 978-0-00-816923-7

10 9 8 7 6 5 4 3 2

Printed in China by RR Donnelley APS Co Ltd.

Collins Bartholomew, the UK's leading independent geographical information
supplier, can provide a digital, custom, and premium mapping service to a
variety of markets.
For further information:
Tel: +44 (0)208 307 4515
e-mail: collinsbartholomew@harpercollins.co.uk

Visit our websites at:
www.collins.co.uk
www.collinsbartholomew.com

If you would like to comment on any aspect of this book,
please contact us at the above address or online.
e-mail: collinsmaps@harpercollins.co.uk

**MIX**
**Paper from**
**responsible sources**
**FSC™ C007454**

FSC™ is a non-profit international organisation established to promote the
responsible management of the world's forests. Products carrying the FSC
label are independently certified to assure consumers that they come from
forests that are managed to meet the social, economic and ecological needs
of present and future generations, and other controlled sources.

Find out more about HarperCollins and the environment at
**www.harpercollins.co.uk/green**

# Contents

# Introduction

The Romans were an advanced and in some ways civilised people whose history began hundreds of years before the birth of Christ (BC) and continued well into the first few centuries afterwards (AD).

They had a tremendous influence on the Mediterranean world and beyond. They left their mark all over their Empire so that today we can still see many of their roads, walls, towns, theatres, and temples. Although the Roman language of Latin is no longer spoken, it forms the basis of many modern languages spoken over the world today.
Some of today's laws are even based on Roman laws.

**Latins settle around the Tiber**
**1000** BC

**Romans get rid of kings and form a republic**
**510** BC

**Burning of Carthage, end of Punic Wars**
**149** BC

**First of Punic wars against Carthage**
**264** BC

**Rome has its fir emperor, Augus**
**31** BC

**Rome founded**
**753** BC

**Roman Kingdom**          **Roman Republic**

The Etruscan king Tarquin the Proud was the last king of Rome. He came to power by killing the previous king.

Romans attacked the city of Carthage and burned it. Then they rounded up the people and sold them as slaves.

mperor Agrippa
efeats the Picts
in Scotland
AD 84

Plague sweeps through the
southern Empire
AD 165

Rome has 20 emperors
murdered one after
the other
AD 235 – 285

Christianity becomes
official religion of Rome
AD 300

Eastern Empire
falls to the Turks
AD 1453

oman Empire

Hadrian is best known for
building a boundary wall across
rthern England to keep the Celts out.

In AD 455, a tribe
called the Vandals
destroyed Roman buildings
and stole property.

# Roman myths

Throughout history stories have been passed down from one generation to the next, first by word of mouth, and then by being written down. Many of these stories may or may not have bits of the truth in them, but usually they were made up to explain events and things that happened. Stories like these are called **myths**. The story of Romulus and Remus is one such myth and it tells of how Rome was founded. Romans also had many myths about the different gods and goddesses they believed in.

A 16th century fresco of Romulus and Remus, the legendary founders of Rome, with their she-wolf mother.

# The story of Romulus and Remus

Visitors to the ancient city of Rome might wonder at a statue on Capitoline Hill which shows a wolf feeding two baby boys. The story is that these boys, called Romulus and Remus, were brought up by a wolf when they were babies. When they grew up they founded the city of Rome, which was named after Romulus.

## Part folk tale, part myth

The story is that the king of Alba Longa, called Numitor, was defeated and sent away by his younger brother Amulius. Numitor's daughter, Rhea Silna, had two sons whose father was Mars, the God of War. When Amulius found this out he had the babies taken and dropped into the River Tiber to kill them. Luckily his servants put the babies in a cradle which floated away and came to rest amongst reeds. A she-wolf heard their cries and looked after them until a shepherd found them and brought them up.

When the boys grew up they took revenge on their wicked uncle Amulius and killed him. They decided to build and rule their own city in the land where they had grown up. They argued over which of 7 hills it should be built on but Romulus eventually got his way and began to lay out the city walls. Remus made fun of the size of the wall and jumped over it. Some tales say that he killed himself doing this but most say that the brothers then argued and Romulus killed his brother. Romulus continued to build and then rule over his city which he called Rome.

Whatever the truth of the story, Romans marked the 21st April 753 BC as being the date that their city and nation was founded.

Remus making fun of the wall by jumping over it.

A Roman coin from AD 300 which has the picture of Romulus, Remus, and the she-wolf.

A mosaic head showing the poet Virgil who wrote a long poem about Aeneus.

# Links to the Trojan war hero Aeneus

In the first centuries AD, Roman historians linked the story of Romulus and Remus to the great Trojan hero, Aeneus. They liked the idea of their nation being founded on great bravery and the ancient Trojan people. So it is thought that they invented a line of kings from Romulus all the way back to Aeneus. Aeneus was a heroic Trojan prince who escaped from the invaded city of Troy. He travelled far and wide and had many adventures before landing in Italy and marrying a Latin princess. Roman children would have been told that Aeneus, rather than Romulus, was the founder of the Roman nation.

# Roman gods and goddesses

The Romans had many gods and goddesses, many borrowed from the Greeks and some from the regions they were conquering. Romans would pray to different gods at various times, depending on what they wanted to ask for.

## Popular gods

Apart from Earth, the planets in our solar system are named after Roman gods, as are some days and months in English. **Mercury** was the speedy messenger of the gods and was worshipped by travellers and merchants. Blood red **Mars** was named after the god of war. The month of March also gets its name from him. **Jupiter** was the king of the gods. Thunderbolts in the sky were believed to be thrown down by him when he was angry. **Saturn** was the god of farming. Saturday is named after him. **Neptune** was the god of the sea, ruling with a three pronged fork or trident. **Uranus** was the god of the sky.

A popular god for the party-going Romans was **Bacchus**, the god of wine and theatre. His head can still be seen over food markets today.

**Janus** was a god with two faces. The month of January is named after him, one head looking to the old year, the other looking forward to the future one.

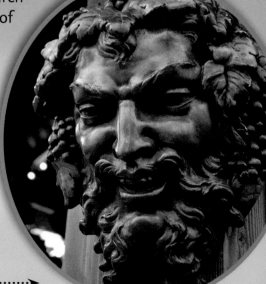

The head of Bacchus at a Christmas market stall.

# Popular goddesses

**Vesta** was the goddess of the home. The Temple of Vesta in Rome always had a flame burning in it. **Diana** was the goddess of hunting and the moon. **Venus** was the goddess of love and beauty. **Minerva** was the goddess of wisdom and learning. Her symbol was an owl. **Ceres** was goddess of the harvest and was often drawn holding a bundle of grain. We call our grain crops 'cereals' after her.

The remains of the Temple of Vesta in Rome.

## Did you know?

The Pantheon was the name given to all of the gods and goddesses together. The temple in Rome was called the Pantheon for worshipping all of them.

Volcanoes are named after **Vulcan**. He combined the Latin god of fire and the Greek god Hephaistos who was a blacksmith. Romans believed that volcanic eruptions were caused by him stirring up his blacksmith's fire too hard.

## Can you identify these gods and goddesses?

# The rise and fall of Rome

The city of Rome grew from settlements amongst the seven hills beside the River Tiber. It held an important geographical position and became the capital of a Roman state first ruled by kings. Then it became the most powerful city in the whole of the vast Roman Empire, first being controlled by elected governors but then by dictators called **emperors**. The Empire lasted for nearly 500 years. After that other powers took control of its western part and Rome was no longer the important city it had once been.

A coloured engraving of the Visigoths invading Rome in AD 410.

# In the beginning

Around 1000 BC, people called the Latins lived in wooden thatched huts in settlements in the seven hills around the river Tiber. Over time these settlements grew to become villages, then towns. A fort was built on the Palatine Hill to protect people and their livestock from attacks by neighbouring tribes. The walled ruins of this fort have been uncovered by archaeologists.

## The three tribes of Rome

Rome is nowadays described as the 'city of seven hills'. Early on in its history neighbouring hills were occupied by other peoples. The Quirinal Hill was settled by the Sabine people. At first there were wars between the Romans and the Sabines but then they joined forces and agreed to live peacefully side by side. Romulus first ruled along with Sabine King Titus Tatius but then ruled alone after Tatius's death.

▲ The remains of the fort on Palatine Hill.

A third hill, the Caelian, was settled by the Luceres who were thought to be Latins and Etruscans. They joined forces with the other people too and the three tribes of Rome made it a very strong and powerful city.

The valley between the hills became a common market place, called the **forum** with a people's meeting place called the **comitium**.

Tiber River (Tiberis)

Field of Mars (Campus Martius)

Capitoline Hill (Collis Capitolinus)

Tiber Island (Insula Tiberina)

Quirinal Hill (Collis Quirinalis)

Viminal Hill (Collis Viminalis)

Roman Forum

Esquiline Hill (Collis Esquilinus)

Colosseum

Palatine Hill (Collis Palatinus)

Caelian Hill (Collis Caelius)

Aventine Hill (Collis Aventinus)

Servian Wall (Murus Servii Tullii)

The seven hills of Rome.

# Etruscan kings

Until about 510 BC Rome was ruled by kings. The last three kings were Etruscan and they made full use of Rome being on a trade route to the Greeks in southern Italy. They passed on the Greek alphabet to the Romans.

The Etruscan peoples ruled the area north of the river Tiber. They were a skilled, civilised people who knew how to plan and build cities and bridges. They also built channels to carry water from one place to another, which they called **aqueducts**.

In Rome they built impressive temples to their gods around a fantastic new square in Rome. They created works of art from stone and bronze and painted beautiful pictures known as **frescoes** on walls. They introduced Romans to chariot races and gladiator fights.

An example of ancient Etruscan art.

# Tarquin the Proud

The very unpopular Etruscan king Tarquin the Proud was the last king of Rome. He came to power by killing the previous king. Eventually the Romans managed to throw him out of the city. He tried to get back in with the help of an Etruscan army from the north but was stopped at a wooden bridge by a hero named Horatio. The Romans destroyed the bridge and Horatio swam back to his own side. After this the Romans decided to have no more kings and rule themselves in an independent republic.

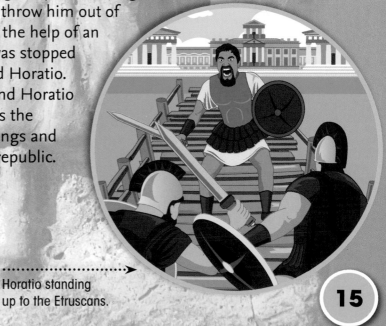

### Did you know?

King Tarquin liked to call himself 'Tarquin Superbus' because he thought he was so superb!

Horatio standing up to the Etruscans.

# The Roman Republic

The word republic comes from the Latin 'res publica' which means 'affairs of the people'. After getting rid of the last of the kings, the Romans decided to rule themselves and so they chose two new governors or **consuls** every year. In 451 BC the rules of the state were decided on and displayed on 12 bronze tablets in the forum. These formed the basis of Roman law for centuries to come.

## Battles all around

The consuls tended to be army generals who led their armies into battles to gain more lands for the Roman State. The neighbouring peoples were not happy about being conquered by Romans so there were lots of terrible wars.

Their main enemies were the Etruscans and also mountain tribes called the Samnites, Aequi, and Volsi. The army of Rome joined forces with other Latin cities to defeat the mountain tribes. They called themselves the 'Latin League'.

Map of the Roman Republic in around 400 BC.

Celts

Etruscans

Umbrians

Corsica

**Roma**

Samnites

Mesapians & Apulians

Romans

Sardinians

Sardinia

Gartha Ginians

Italiotes

Greeks

Sicilia

# The destruction of Rome

In 390 BC the Roman Republic was taken by surprise by an army of Gauls invading from the north. The city of Rome was left in ruins by them and was not properly rebuilt until 50 years later. The Romans built a large wall around the city to defend it from future invasions.

The Gauls attacking Rome.

# The spread of the Roman Republic

After Rome was rebuilt the Romans began to invade other lands again. They captured cities and eventually defeated their nearest enemies, the Gauls and the Etruscans.

If cities surrendered straight away to them they allowed the people to become part of the Roman Republic and share the benefits of being Roman. However, if people tried to put up a fight, they would be killed or captured and made into slaves.

The Roman Republic spread south until Greek cities ruled by King Pyrrhus came into Roman hands. By 264 BC Rome controlled all of Italy.

# Conquering Carthage

The Romans had a large highly-trained army that was trying to make their Empire bigger. They were bound to start fights with the neighbouring Carthaginian Empire. Based in Carthage in North Africa, this rival Empire ruled much of the Western Mediterranean. There were three major wars with the Carthaginians which were called the **Punic Wars**, since the Latin word for Carthaginian was 'punicus'.

## The first Punic War

The first war was over who had control of Sicily. At first the Romans had no chance of winning because the battles needed to be fought at sea and they were up against the powerful Carthaginian navy. The Romans had to learn how to build ships fast and create their own navy. After winning some of their first sea battles, the Romans then lost many of their ships in storms. However Carthage finally let Rome have Sicily, and later the islands of Corsica and Sardinia too.

Map of the Roman Republic and Carthaginian Empire in around 200 BC.

Gauls

Illyrians

Corsica

**Roma**

Celtiberians

Sardinia

*Mare Internum*

Sicilia

**Carthage**

Numidians

Roman Republic

Carthaginian Empire

# The war with the elephants

The second war started over who should control Spain and its trade routes. Famously the Carthaginian General Hannibal led an army of 35 000 men and 37 elephants across the Pyrenees and then the Alps so they could surprise the Romans by attacking from the north. Despite losing a third of his army and all but one elephant in the mountains, Hannibal's plan worked and he defeated the Roman armies in Italy.

However the Romans got their own back by invading Spain and attacking Carthage in North Africa, forcing Hannibal to return to defend his home city. The Roman General Scipio defeated Hannibal at the battle of Zuma. Rome then took Spain for its own Empire.

# The burning of Carthage

In 149 BC the Romans attacked the city of Carthage and burned it. Then they rounded up the people and sold them as slaves.

They also conquered Southern Gaul (France today) and all Greek lands. The Roman Republic was in control of all Mediterranean countries.

Map of the Roman Republic in around 100 BC.

Gaul

Spain

Corsica

Roma

Sardinia

Macedonia

Greece

Asia Minor

Mare Internum

Sicilia

Carthage

Africa

Cyprus

☐ Roman Republic

# Julius Caesar

Born in 100 BC, Julius Caesar is perhaps one of the most famous Roman leaders. He was a rising star at a time when there was great unrest in Rome. He was a very clever politician and a powerful and ruthless army general. In 49 BC he became a dictator (an unelected leader) of the state of Rome. This marked the end of the Roman Republic.

## Celebrity status

Caesar was well known and very popular. He was once captured by pirates and made them raise the amount of money asked for his ransom! When he was freed he organised the navy to capture and kill the pirates.

He also had great success as an army general invading other countries and expanding Roman territory. He conquered northern Gaul and led armies into Britain and Germany.

### Caesar quotes

**'Divide et impera!' – ('Divide and conquer')**
Caesar used this method of beating his enemies. He made them fight amongst themselves then it was easier to beat them.

**'Alea Iacta est' – ('The die is cast')**
This means that once an action is taken, there is no going back. Caesar said this when he led his army across the River Rubicon on the way to take over Rome as a dictator.

**'Veni, vidi, vici' – ('I came, I saw, I conquered')**
This is how Caesar described his quick victory at Zela in 47 BC.

# Famous face, famous name

Julius Caesar was the first man to have his face and neck put onto a coin. Even in modern times his face still appears on stamps. The famous playwright William Shakespeare even wrote a play about him.

## Did you know?

The word 'caesar' came to mean ruler in other languages. In German it became 'kaiser' and in Russian 'czar'. Many of the Roman emperors called themselves Caesar followed by their own names.

# The Julian calendar

In 46 BC Caesar consulted with astronomers and changed the way the calendar was organised. Until then it had been based on the cycles of the moon but that did not work very well. Caesar changed it so that it was based on how long the Earth takes to go around the sun. He gave a year 365 days. He made every fourth year a 'leap year' adding an extra day to February to keep the calendar working correctly. We still base modern calendars on this one. The month of July was named after Julius.

# Murderous times

When Caesar became a dictator he showed off his power by holding a massive killing circus. Hundreds of **gladiators** (trained killers) fought each other to death in front of crowds of cheering people. Hundreds of animals were killed too. It let his people see how powerful he was.

Caesar stayed a peoples' favourite because he was a strong leader and did things to help the poor. However, other politicians and even his friends were afraid of his power and they plotted to kill him. On 15th March 44 BC he was stabbed 23 times on the steps of the senate.

Caesar turned to someone he thought was his friend and said his famous last words: 'Et tu, Brute?' meaning, 'And you, Brutus?'

21

# The Roman Empire

Julius Caesar's dictatorship had already marked the end of the Roman Republic. From then on it would not be ruled by elected consuls but by emperors. The first emperor was to be Julius Caesar's nephew Octavian, but not until more battles and bloodshed had taken place.

## Octavian, Antony, and Lepidus

After struggling to be accepted as a consul by the senate, Octavian fought and defeated Caesar's friend Mark Antony. He was still not allowed power, so he joined forces with Antony and Lepidus to bring armies into Rome to defeat those against them and seize power.

Lepidus let Octavian and Antony share the rule of Roman lands. Octavian controlled the western part and Antony controlled the eastern part.

A map of the Roman Empire at its largest in AD 117.

# Antony and Cleopatra

Mark Antony went to Egypt where he fell in love with Queen Cleopatra and lived with her for ten years. Antony and Cleopatra are a very well-known couple in history and William Shakespeare also wrote a play about them.

Meanwhile Octavian grew more and more popular as a leader in Rome. In 31 BC he went to war against Mark Antony's forces and defeated him in a battle at sea, before taking over Egypt.

Mark Antony then stabbed himself, and Cleopatra is said to have allowed herself to be bitten by a poisonous snake so that she too would die.

A painting showing the death of Cleopatra.

## Did you know?

Cleopatra was famous far and wide for her great beauty. She is said to have bathed daily in donkeys' milk.

# Emperor Augustus

The Senate made Octavian the leader of all the Roman world and renamed him Augustus which means 'great and much respected'. He was also given the title of **imperator**, meaning emperor. After all the battling for power Emperor Caesar Augustus went on to rule peacefully and wisely.

A statue of the Emperor Augustus.

23

# Famous Roman leaders

Some of the emperors who followed Augustus made names for themselves because of the good things they did, whilst others were famous for bad things. We know about them today because of what was written about them by Roman writers and historians.

## Tiberius AD 14-37

Although the Romans were enjoying a time of peace during his rule, the Emperor Tiberius was hated and feared. He spent the last ten years of his life on the island of Capri. It is said that he had his enemies thrown off the cliffs there.

### Did you know?

Caligula was the nickname of Emperor Gaius and it meant 'little soldier boots' like those he wore as a child.

## Caligula AD 37-41

At first the Romans were pleased to have a new emperor. But Caligula was even madder and crueller than Tiberius. He was said to be very hairy and anyone staring at him or saying the word 'goat' in front of him was executed. It is also said that he used to dress up as the gods and tried to get his favourite horse made a consul in the senate! After just four years as emperor he was murdered.

# Claudius AD 41-54

Claudius was the nephew of Caligula and turned out to be a good and wise emperor. He sent the Roman army away to conquer Celtic tribes and extend the Empire into Britain. Claudius died after being given poisoned mushrooms to eat.

GOLD COIN: FOUND AT BREDGAR

CLAUDIUS 24

This stamp shows a gold coin with the head of Claudius on it.

# Nero AD 54-68

Emperor Nero was also thought to be totally mad. He threw people in the sewers if they refused to call him god. He liked to pick fights with people and then kill them.

Nero used to play his lyre and sing, forcing his audience to sit through long and not always enjoyable performances.

Emperor Nero killed two of his wives, his stepbrother and his own mother. In the end the army came to kill him. He tried to kill himself, but a servant had to do it for him.

# Hadrian AD 117-138

Hadrian was also known as one of the good emperors. He loved travelling and is best known for building a boundary wall across northern Britain to keep the Celts out. There are still some parts of Hadrian's Wall that can be seen today.

THE HAPPINESS OF YOUR LIFE DEPENDS UPON THE QUALITY OF YOUR THOUGHTS.

MARCUS AURELIUS

# Marcus Aurelius AD 161-180

Marcus Aurelius was a fair ruler and tried to do his best for his people. He is best known for books he wrote about philosophy, that is, thoughts about life.

# The Romans in Britain

Emperor Claudius's army began conquering the Celtic tribes of Britain in AD 43. General Agricola completed the invasion as far as the northeast of Scotland in AD 84. The new Roman province was called **Britannia** and became part of the Roman Empire for the next 400 years. The Romans called the natives **Barbarians**, meaning strangers.

## Queen Boudicca

In AD 60 Queen Boudicca led a big battle against the Romans. She managed to gather together an army of 100 000 Celtic warriors.

Although only 10 000 Roman soldiers went into battle against the huge Celtic army, the Roman soldiers won because they were far more organised and better trained.

The statue of Boudicca in London.

## Roman language

One important result of the Roman invasion was that the Romans introduced the British people to reading and writing. The Romans scraped words on wax-covered wooden tablets. If any Celts wanted to become Roman citizens they could join the army or get a government job but they had to learn Latin, the Roman language. A lot of Latin words are found in the English language today and Roman numerals can still be seen on clocks and watches.

# Clues from the past

Archaeologists have found coins, pottery, and many other clues about Roman life in Britain. From old pollen grains they can tell that wheat and barley were the main crops. They can tell from old bones that people ate cattle, sheep, chickens, duck, geese, and goats. They have even found grape pips which make them think that the Romans may have tried to make wine in Britain.

The Romans brought coins into Britain and began to use money to buy and sell goods. Many trades were started up such as building, pottery, buying and selling farm foods, and mining for metals.

# Roman towns

The Romans told the Celtic tribes to live in and around towns and allowed them to rule themselves as a way to make them more 'civilised'. Many towns had walls built around them for defence and for show.

Towns in England with names ending in '-chester', '-caster' or '-cester' are built on sites of Roman camps or forts, although the Romans would have had different names for them. London was called 'Londinium' and the city of Bath is named after its Roman baths.

# Roads and walls

The Romans built about 16 000 km (10 000 miles) of roads in Britain and some roads today follow the same routes. Two main walls were built in the north to keep out the rival tribes and mark the edge of the Empire – Hadrian's Wall in northern England and the Antonine Wall in central Scotland.

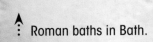
Roman baths in Bath.

# The fall of Rome

The 'fall of Rome' refers to the hundred or more years leading up to the end of the Roman Empire. During this time the Empire became very unstable and weak and there were invasions by other tribes.

## The Empire loses strength

In AD 165 the Roman armies returned from conquering the east but brought the plague back with them, which led to great loss of life in the Roman population. After that there was a fifty-year period with over 20 emperors, each murdered in turn. No one could decide who should rule and this led to a lot of fighting between Romans.

## The Empire splits

In the third century, a tribe called the Huns invaded northern Gaul from eastern Europe. They forced other tribes, like the Visigoths, into the Roman Empire. In AD 395 the Empire was split into West and East and the West then became overrun by Barbarians. In AD 451 the Roman army defeated Attila the Hun and his army in northern Gaul. This was to be the Roman army's last victory.

Attila the Hun may have looked something like this.

# Invasions

In AD 401 the Visigoths invaded Milan and Emperor Honorius was forced out of his home. Then in AD 410 they invaded Italy again and the Roman army was called back from other parts of its Empire (like Britain) to try and defend Rome. It was too late, Rome was open to attack. In AD 455, a tribe called the Vandals destroyed Roman buildings and stole property. In AD 476, the last Roman emperor, strangely enough called Romulus like the founder of Rome, was pushed out into exile. By the end of the fourth century the Western Roman Empire no longer existed.

## The Eastern Empire/ Byzantine Empire

Constantinople is now called Istanbul.

An Empire in the east called Byzantine continued for another 1000 years. The capital city was Constantinople and had been founded and named after Emperor Constantine some years before. He called the city the 'New Rome of the East'. The Byzantine Empire was an important trading Empire and centre of culture.

Mare Germanicum

Oceanus Atlanticus

Italia
Corsica
Roma
Macedonia
Pontus Euxinus
Constantinople
Sardinia
Mare Internum
Sicilia
Achaia
Asia
Africa
Cyprus

A map of the Byzantine Empire at its largest in AD 628.

# Roman warfare

The Roman Empire could never have grown so big and powerful had it not had such a large Roman army. This army was led by experts in warfare and the soldiers were equipped with excellent weapons.

Army generals had brilliant military tactics and had highly trained and organised soldiers under their command. They could even defeat enemies with armies ten times the size of theirs.

A stone carving from AD 260 shows a Roman battle scene.

# Roman army

The Roman army was a brutal and powerful force. At its largest it had about half a million soldiers based in all corners of the Empire. The army did not just win battles to make the Empire bigger, it built roads, bridges, and canals to connect places in one part of the Empire to another as well. Roman soldiers also built towns, forts, and walls.

## Legions

The army was split into 30 **legions**. Each legion had between 4000 and 6000 soldiers. Each legion was then divided up into 10 **cohorts**, which contained six **centuries** of about 80 **legionaries** (the best Roman soldiers) plus some auxiliary soldiers. Centuries were led by **centurions**, who carried canes (short sticks) to show their importance and to beat their men

Each legion had its own flags or **standards** to march behind, including one with the name and symbol of the legion. The soldier carrying the standard wore an animal head and skin over his head. Each legion had a standard with the image of the emperor on it and a spear-shaped standard made up of discs and with a hand sign at the top. Legions also had a horn player called the **cornicen** to sound out battle signals.

An onager

# Weapons

The army had many weapons to use against the enemy. Soldiers were trained to use javelins with metal tips. These broke off when hitting their target so that the javelins could not be picked up and thrown back. Soldiers were also trained to use swords and daggers.

However, before any hand-to-hand combat took place, the army would use giant catapults called **onagers** to fire rocks or burning tar balls to weaken enemy defences.

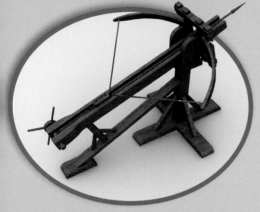

The Roman soldiers also used large crossbows called **ballistas** to fire arrows.

# Clever tactics

The Roman army was able to beat armies ten times their size by using cleverly planned out battle tactics. They fought in standards lines with their shields facing the enemy.

If attacked from above, the Roman soldiers went into **testudos** (which means 'like a tortoise') formations, and held their shields over their heads.

A Roman standard showing the Eagle, which was the symbol of the Roman army.

# Roman soldiers

Only men and male Roman citizens could join the Roman army. Joining up meant 25 years of travel, adventure, learning fighting skills and hopefully getting some battle glory. Soldiers also learned to do another job such as record keeping, building, engineering, and nursing.

## Fit foot soldiers

Roman soldiers had to be extremely fit as they could be expected to march up to 30 km (18 miles) a day. This might also be with all their kit on their backs including weapons, tools, and cooking utensils.

Every day soldiers would exercise by running, walking, or swimming. They would practise using their swords and javelins.

Soldiers were paid and had to buy their own uniform and kit.

# Discipline

The army had very strict rules. Soldiers were severely punished or even killed for disobeying orders. If a soldier fell asleep on guard duty he could be put out of the safety of the fort for a night.

If a whole legion went against orders then sometimes lots were drawn and 1 out of every 10 soldiers was clubbed to death by the other 9. General Crassus did this to his troops when they lost a battle. It was called **decimation**.

Soldiers were well rewarded too. They were paid well and some money was kept aside for their pensions. Soldiers were allowed to keep any treasure they took as well as some prisoners to sell as slaves. They received various types of crowns as rewards for bravery.

When they retired soldiers would be given some land to live on.

A Roman helmet and wreath.
·············>

# Auxiliary soldiers

Sometimes the army recruited soldiers from the armies they had conquered. Soldiers who had not yet become Roman citizens could be trained as auxiliary soldiers. They were paid less the Roman soldiers and were often sent to fight in the front lines of battle where it was more dangerous.

# Roman camps and forts

In the earlier years of the Empire the army was on the move a lot. They carried everything they needed with them and would set up camp overnight. Later on forts were built when soldiers needed to spend time in one place while they were either building towns or defending the edges of the Empire.

## Setting up camp

The first thing the soldiers had to do when setting up camp was to dig out a defensive ditch all around the outside of the camp. Then the dug-out earth would be formed into a wall or **rampart** and strengthened with wooden stakes. Inside the camp the tents would be put up in neat rows. Soldiers would then eat and rest. The next morning the tents would be taken down and the equipment packed up, ready to be carried on to the next stopping point.

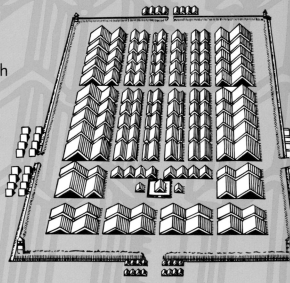

A bird's eye view of a Roman camp.

A Roman camp created for a 'Roman festival' in Moscow.

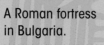
A Roman fortress in Bulgaria.

# Forts

We know a lot about what Roman forts looked like as their remains can be found in many countries today.

Some stone structures are still standing and in some places the forts have been reconstructed from the ruins.

The ruins of a Roman fort on Hadrian's Wall in England.

# Diagram of a fort

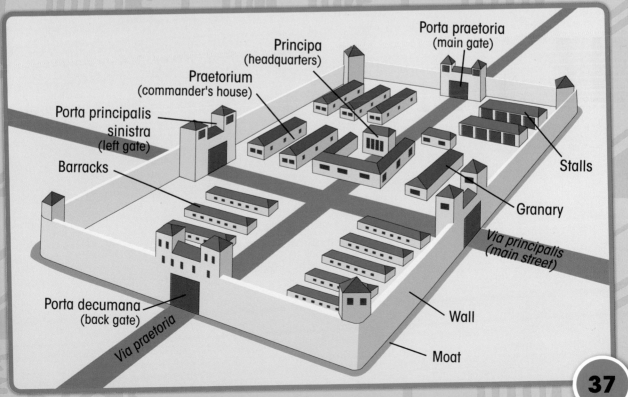

Porta praetoria (main gate)

Principa (headquarters)

Praetorium (commander's house)

Porta principalis sinistra (left gate)

Barracks

Stalls

Granary

Via principalis (main street)

Porta decumana (back gate)

Via praetoria

Wall

Moat

37

# Roman pastimes

Romans often had a lot of leisure time because slaves did their work for them. A daily pastime was a trip to the bath house to bathe and relax with friends. They also loved a day out at the chariot races or at the amphitheatre. Bloodthirsty Romans enjoyed watching gruesome animal and gladiator fights. They also enjoyed going to watch funny or sad plays at open-air theatres.

Roman baths in Bath, England.

# Chariot racing

Just as today people find motor sport an exciting and dangerous sport to watch, the same was true for the Romans with chariot racing. Up to twelve riders each stood on their chariots pulled by horses and raced seven laps round a track. The first chariot over the line was the winner, whether or not the rider had managed to stay in the chariot!

## The Circus Maximus

The main stadium or **hippodrome** in Rome was the 'Circus Maximus'. Circus was the Roman word for race track and maximus means very big. It was three times the size of a modern-day sports stadium and could seat up to 250 000 people. Spectators were men, women, and children from every social class. The poorest people had to stand high up at the back of the stadium and the rich senators got marble seating with a trackside view. There could be as many as twenty-four races a day and people liked to bet on the winners.

The corners are always the most exciting part of any race track.

Ruins of the Circus Maximus in Rome.

spina

race track

# Races

In the middle of the track there would have been a long platform or **spina** where the officials stood. At each end were three tree-sized pillars like giant upside-down decorated ice cream cones.

Each race started with a trumpet blast and the dropping of a white flag. Huge dolphin figures were used to mark the laps.

Usually two or four horses pulled the chariots, but sometimes six or eight horses would be used to add to the danger and the excitement.

The Roman race track 'Spina'.

A chariot race demonstration at a 'Roman Show' in Jordan.

### Did you know?

Chariot races first took place to celebrate 'Holy Days'. People took time away from normal daily life to go to the races. This is why we call our days off 'holidays'.

## Four teams

Spectators had four teams they could support: red, green, white, or blue. Fans would chant and shout for their team and sometimes there were fights between rival supporters.

## The racing drivers

Many of the chariot riders were slaves, but some were professional riders who got paid for racing. Many did not race past the age of twenty as they would be badly injured or killed. Winning riders got prize money and a victory palm branch to wave. They also became celebrities if they won, like today's Formula One racing drivers.

Some racing drivers tied themselves to the chariot with the long reins. They carried daggers to cut themselves free in case they were trapped by an overturned chariot.

The Etruscans introduced chariot racing to the Romans. They had found out about the sport from the Greeks.

# Gladiators

Gladiators were trained fighters, mostly men, who fought as a way of entertaining crowds of spectators in huge arenas called **amphitheatres**. Many were slaves, but some were paid volunteers. They could earn fame and fortune by winning lots of fights. True gladiators did not normally fight to the death as most fights were stopped when one of them was wounded or too exhausted. Winners were given prize money and a victory crown. Some gladiator slaves managed to win their freedom by pleasing the emperor with their fighting skills.

# Types of gladiators

The different types of gladiators were named after the armour and weapons they used. For example:

**secatores** had swords and shields

**reticarii** had nets and a trident

**dimachaeri** had a sword in each hand

**laqueatores** had ropes

# When did gladiator fights start?

The first gladiator fights were held at funerals by the Greeks and later the Etruscans because it was thought that blood on a grave helped the soul of a dead person. At first the dead person's enemy would be killed, but later on any two fighters would be made to fight to the death. Then gladiator fights began to take place in market places and other open spaces just for sport. By 110 BC gladiator fights were a popular spectator sport and special arenas were built. The biggest arena ever built was the Colosseum in Rome in AD 80.

To make it more interesting for the spectators, the different types of gladiators would have to fight each other.

# Spartacus

Spartacus was a gladiator famous for leading a huge slave rebellion in Rome. This was when thousands of slaves escaped and went around Italy fighting battles. Despite having some success in battle, they never managed to take over Rome and were eventually defeated. Those who were captured alive were crucified (put to death by being nailed to trees or crosses).

# Roman baths

Most Romans went to the baths (bath houses) every day. For them they were not just a place to bathe and get clean, but more like a social trip to a leisure centre! They were great places to meet with friends and catch up with all the gossip. As well as taking dips in the different pools, they could also exercise and play games. Food, wine, and entertainment were provided as well.

## Underfloor heating

Roman engineers invented central heating. At homes and at the baths they heated air and water using underfloor furnaces. Whilst Roman citizens relaxed in comfort above ground, teams of slaves kept the furnaces burning below ground.

Men and women bathed at different times. For women it was usually in the mornings and for men it was in the afternoons.

It was hot tiring work for the slaves to keep the furnaces burning.

# Baths in every town

Baths were so important to the Romans that they were built in every town throughout the Empire. We know this because remains of them have been found in all corners of the Empire.

These are archaeological ruins of ancient Roman baths in Beirut, Lebanon. The pillars were below the floor and let hot air move around to heat up the pools. Pipes also moved hot air around inside the walls.

A view of the Roman Baths in Bath, Britain.

# Different rooms

At the baths there were many different rooms, for example:

**frigidarium** – a cold room with a cold pool

**caldarium** – a hot room with a hot bath

**tepidarium** – a warm room

**apodyterium** – a heated changing room

**natatio** – an outdoor pool

**palaestra** – an open-air courtyard for exercising

This ancient Roman frigidarium is in Pompeii, Italy. The remains of a colourful wall mosaic can be seen.

45

# Drama in Roman times

The Greek tradition of plays performed in large semi-circular open-air theatres was adopted by the Romans in the third century BC. Then there were either funny plays known as **comedies**, or sad plays known as **tragedies**. At first the Romans translated the Greek plays but later on they wrote their own.

## The first pantomimes

Over time the longer, more complicated plays were performed for more educated people. For the less educated people the speeches were cut out of plays and replaced by singing and miming. Song and mime performances were called **pantomimes**.

## Masks and costumes

Masks and costumes helped audiences identify characters more easily from far away.

The first Roman actors were all men and they wore masks to show different character types. The men wore pale masks to perform as women. Different colours of costumes were used to show different types of characters. For example, red was used to show a poor person, purple a rich person, and white an old person.

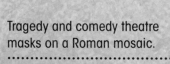

Tragedy and comedy theatre masks on a Roman mosaic.

# Theatres

At first theatres were temporary wooden structures which could be put up and pulled down quickly for festivals or holy days. However, as plays became more and more popular, more permanent open-air structures were built from stone. They were generally built in the same style, with a large background wall and stage, then rows of stone seating.

The ruins of the Roman theatre in Aosta, Italy.

An ancient Roman theatre at Miletus in Turkey.

# Actors

Acting was not seen as being a very respectable job so it was left to slaves or freemen to do. In later times women were allowed to take part in mimes and masks were no longer used. At the height of the Roman Empire, plays were written for mass audiences and dramas became more like real life. Some plays were very rude, others were extremely violent. One time an actor swapped places with a criminal who was then tortured and killed on stage.

# Audiences

Audiences would clap if they enjoyed a performance just like we do today. If they snapped their fingers that meant it was just alright, and if they waved a white hankie or part of their toga they were delighted with it.

At one time women in the audience were not allowed to sit too close to the stage in case they ran off with some of the actors!

# Building Rome

There is a well-known saying, 'Rome wasn't built in a day' which means that it takes time to do something important well.

The Romans knew how to do things well and in a way that would last. They found a way of making very strong concrete and cement and they also had highly skilled engineers and builders. As a result, many of the towns, roads, aqueducts, ancient bath houses, temples, and theatres that were built in Roman times can still be seen today.

An ancient Roman
aqueduct in Istanbul, Turkey.

# Roman houses

Romans knew how to make a strong, long-lasting cement and were able to make their houses out of bricks. In the cities well-off people lived in large family houses, but poorer people lived in crowded blocks of flats. In the countryside the rich lived in big houses called **villas**, but the poor lived in simple wooden cottages.

## Town house

A large town house or **dormus** was built in a rectangle shape using stone, cement, and wood. It had an entrance hall called an **atrium** with an open skylight above it. It might also have had a pool. At the front entrance to the street there could be shops on either side. At the back of the house would be a garden courtyard. Roofs were gently sloping and tiled. Some houses had glass windows, but the glass was green and rather dim. Most houses would have wooden shutters or animal skins at the windows.

Diagram of a large Roman family house.

timber

compluvium (an unroofed space over the atrium, through which rain fell and was collected)

tiles

fresco

tablinum (study/office)

impluvium (pool)

atrium

vestibule

shop

peristyle (columns)

garden

dining room

kitchen

latrines (toilets)

bed chamber

mosaic

# Country villas

Even today we still call large houses in the country 'villas'. We know what Roman villas were like as some are still standing today, thanks to the strength of Roman cement. Also, although we do not have photographs from Roman times, we do have their paintings and mosaics. Villas were very grand houses, often with large columns and arches.

A Roman mosaic showing a country villa.

A sketch of a Roman villa.

## Did you know?

Today a mansion is a large private house, but in Roman times 'mansions' were inns by the roadsides where travellers could rest, bathe, eat, sleep, and change their horses.

This is a villa in Pompeii, Italy. A large part of Pompeii was covered and preserved under ash after Mount Vesuvius erupted in AD 76.

# Roman interiors

When the ruins of the ancient Roman towns of Herculaneum and Pompeii were uncovered, it was discovered that many of the interiors of houses had not been too damaged. This means that people today have been able to learn how Roman houses were laid out and what the insides looked like.

## Features of Roman houses

Most Roman houses had courtyards and atriums. Inside they might have had a pool. They would all have had a shrine to their household gods and spirits called the 'genii loci'. Family members would worship at the altars in mornings and at mealtimes.

Houses had central heating systems called **hypocausts**. Furnaces were lit below the houses which heated up the air beneath the floors.

Wealthy families had their own baths and toilets. However the people living in flats and terraced houses had to use public toilets. For men these were often clay pots out in the street! Ordinary people went to the baths daily to keep clean.

The courtyard of a ruined villa at the ancient Roman town of Pompeii.

This house has **fresco** paintings on the walls. It also has a shrine to the household gods.

# Mosaics

Mosaics are pictures made from lots of coloured stones or tiles cemented into floors or walls. They were very popular in Roman times and tell us a lot about Roman life.

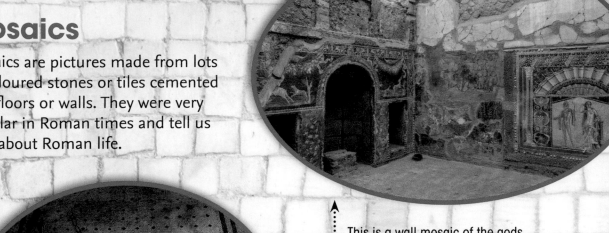

This is a wall mosaic of the gods Neptune and Amphitrite which was found in a Herculaneum villa.

A tourist walking around the Bardo museum in Tunisia, which has a world-famous collection of Roman mosaics and a lot of Roman treasure.

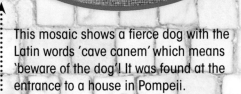

This mosaic shows a fierce dog with the Latin words 'cave canem' which means 'beware of the dog'! It was found at the entrance to a house in Pompeii.

A mosaic from the Roman era, found in Turkey.

# The Colosseum

The Colosseum was originally called the Flavian amphitheatre. It was, however, a colossal building and soon the nickname stuck. It was the largest open-air stadium in the Roman Empire and could seat up to 50 000 spectators. It was built in the centre of Rome by order of the Emperor Vespasium and took ten years to build, completed in AD 80. For 500 years Roman emperors put on extravagant but barbaric shows about 90 times a year. They wanted to show off their power and feed the bloodthirsty tastes of 'the mob'.

Much of the Colosseum still stands to this day, and tourists come from all over the world to see it.

# A day at the Colosseum

A day at the Colosseum began with grand parades of gladiators, musicians, dancers, jugglers, and priests. Then, in the mornings there would be wild animal hunts, performing animals, and fights between animals. Gladiator fights took place in the afternoons.

During the Roman Empire about one million animals were killed in the Colosseum arena. Emperor Trajan had 11 000 animals killed just to celebrate winning a war.

The wide exit tunnel was called the **vomitorium**. There were also **aqueducts** leading to the arena so that the stage could be flooded and pretend sea battles could be performed by gladiators.

## Above ground

Above ground there were four levels of arcades and rows of seating. Women had to sit in the back rows away from the men. The wealthiest senators and the emperor had the best seats towards the front. The arena itself had hidden trap doors under a sand-covered floor and often had fancy staging and scenery on it.

## Below ground

Under the ground was a maze of passageways, tunnels, holding pens, and cages for humans and wild animals. Some animals were starved and tormented so that they would be hungry and fierce when let loose in the arena. Lifts were used to carry animals or prisoners up into the arena.

When they were inside the Colosseum, spectators would have had no idea of everything going on beneath the arena.

## Did you know?

For hundreds of years the Romans fed Christians, as well as criminals, to the wild animals. When Emperor Constantine accepted the Christian religion this soon stopped.

# Roman towns

A lot is now known about the way Roman towns were laid out because some towns today were originally built at the time of the Empire. A fantastic glimpse of life in Roman towns has been given by the discovery of Pompeii and Herculaneum. These towns lay buried under volcanic ash until excavation started in the mid-18th century.

## Common features of towns

Roman towns were commonly laid out in a rough rectangular shape and had a grid pattern of roads and streets. Most towns would have been surrounded by four walls with four gates or **portae** in each. Visiting traders would have to pay a fee or **toll** to get into the city. The walls often had turrets at the corners which were for defence and also for decoration. Each town had a central market place called a **forum**. Roman towns also had shops, bakeries, bars, laundries, baths, temples, and, of course, lots of houses.

Tourists visit the ancient town of Pompeii, with its original roads and buildings.

A Roman wall and gate in Barcelona, Spain.

# Shopping, eating, and drinking

Towns had many shops and markets just as we do today. People met up at the shops, theatres, baths, and laundries. When they wanted to have a drink or a snack they could call in at a bar, where wine was kept cool in large stone jars. There were over 120 snack bars in Pompeii.

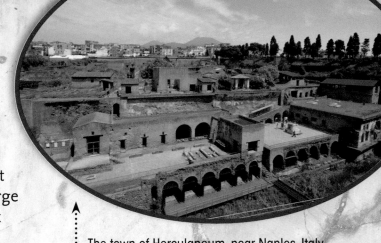

The town of Herculaneum, near Naples, Italy.

This photo shows a bar in Pompeii. The tops of large stone wine jars can be seen along the bar tops.

The remains of a laundry in Pompeii.

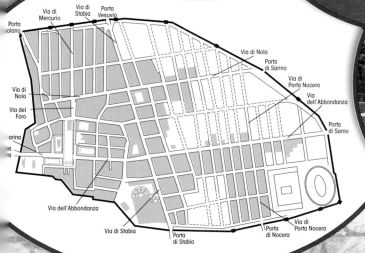

A plan of Pompeii.

Porta olano
Via di Mercurio
Via di Stabia
Porta Vesuvio
Via di Nola
Porta di Sarino
Via di Porta Nocera
Via dell'Abbondanza
Via di Nola
Via del Foro
arina
Porta di Sarno
Via dell'Abbondanza
Via di Stabia
Porta di Stabia
Porta di Nocera
Via di Porta Nocera

A view of Pompeii ruins, looking towards a **colonnade**, (a row of pillars or columns) which would have had shops and market stalls in it.

# Roman roads, bridges, and aqueducts

The Romans were such remarkable engineers and builders that many of the structures and roads they built have not only survived 2000 years but are still in use today. Bridges and aqueducts are as impressive now as they were in Roman times.

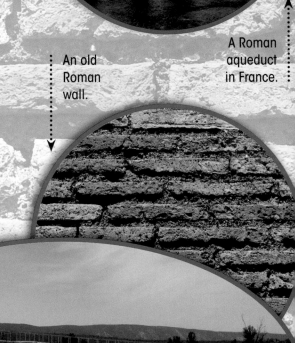

A Roman aqueduct in France.

An old Roman wall.

## Roman concrete

One of the reasons that Romans were able to build such amazingly strong structures was their concrete called **pozzolana**. The special ingredient in this concrete was a powdery volcanic ash which was added to lime and water. As well as hardening in the air, this concrete could also set under water. This made it ideal for building bridges, harbours, and aqueducts.

An old Roman bridge in France.

# 'All roads lead to Rome'

Before they built their roads, the Romans put down foundations of clay, chalk, or gravel. If the ground was boggy they would lay down bundles of sticks and sheepskins to stop the road from sinking. Then they would lay bigger, flat stones for the road surface. Roads would have gentle slopes from the middle to a ditch at each side so that rain water could run off.

The Via Appia was a main route into Rome.

# Aqueducts

Romans built hundreds of miles of aqueducts to carry fresh clean water from springs in the countryside into towns and cities. The water flowed along because there were very slight slopes in the aqueducts.

The city of Rome alone needed a billion litres of clean water every day. The Virginie aqueduct, most of which is underground, is still in use today.

Romans also had very fancy and clever sewage systems built.

## Did you know?

The Romans buried their dead along roadsides out of town. This was so the ghosts of the dead could not find their way back in.

This is the bridge over the River Tiber in Rome. Bridge builders were important people in Roman society.

The water channel in the Tomar Aqueduct can clearly be seen.

# Roman customs

Many of the customs in Roman times were similar to those today. Like people nowadays, the Romans valued education and there were private tutors or schools for those who could afford it.

Fashion, jewellery, and personal appearance were also important to the Romans. The type of clothes worn showed a person's rank and how much money they had.

Food played an big part in Roman times. The pizzas and pastas which many of us enjoy today had their origins in Roman times. However many foods that we take for granted today were not known then.

J. Williamson

A Roman feast.

# Roman education

In Roman times education was thought to be very important but only the rich could afford to pay for it. Schools were only in cities or towns. Sometimes children had a slave tutor, called a **paedagogus**. Teachers were often Greek, since Greek education was very highly thought of.

## Primary, secondary, and college

Primary school was for 7 to 12 year olds. Boys and girls mostly learned 'the three rs': reading, 'riting and 'rithmetic.

From age 12 to 16 pupils learned Greek and Latin language and literature, mathematics, geography, history, astronomy, science, music, and athletics. As girls were old enough to marry at the age of 12, it was mostly boys who went to secondary school.

If boys wanted a career in politics or an important position in society they would go to college and learn how to give speeches.

Schools only had 10 to 12 pupils in a class.

A Roman stone carving of students with books and a teacher.

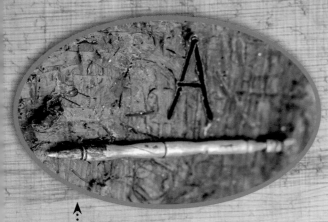

Children practised their letters and numbers on wax tablets.

# Reading and writing

Young children first practised the alphabet on wax tablets. A sharp metal point on their **stylus** scraped the letters or numerals. They often had to copy out proverbs. Girls were not encouraged in their reading as much as boys. The poet Juvenal wrote, 'I hate a woman who reads.' The Roman alphabet is used to write many modern day languages, including the words you are reading now!

Later on pupils learned to write with ink on scrolls made from animal skins or a type of paper called **papyrus**. They would learn to read from scrolls too.

Teachers could be very strict and punish lazy children with beatings. In secondary school pupils could be whipped.

| Roman numerals | |
| --- | --- |
| I | 1 |
| II | 2 |
| III | 3 |
| IV | 4 |
| V | 5 |
| VI | 6 |
| VII | 7 |
| VIII | 8 |
| IX | 9 |
| X | 10 |
| XI | 11 |
| XII | 12 |
| etc | |
| XX | 20 |
| XXX | 30 |
| XXXX | 40 |
| L | 50 |
| LX | 60 |
| XC | 90 |
| C | 100 |
| D | 500 |
| M | 1000 |

# Hard maths

Roman numerals were hard to do sums with. Also there was no symbol for zero, so this made things even more difficult.

Can you do this sum?
**VI + XXX + XIV**
The answer should be **L**.

Sometimes a calculator was used for a difficult sum – not an electronic one, but a counter called an **abacus** (right).

# Roman clothes

If asked to name what Romans wore, most people would answer togas. However most ordinary people wore simple woollen tunics with holes for the arms and head. Belts were worn around the waist.

## Togas

Togas were only really worn for special occasions and ceremonies unless you were a senator or the emperor. They were large semi-circular cloths, three times the length of the person wearing them and made from wool or silk. They were wrapped around the body leaving the right arm uncovered. In cold weather a heavy woollen cloak was draped over the back and fastened at the front with a pin or brooch.

Togas were usually white, but senators had purple borders on theirs and boys wore ones with deep red borders.

## Tunics

Tunics were worn by everyone in Roman times. Ordinary people or **plebeians** and slaves wore dark-coloured or brown knee-length tunics. Most were made of wool, but some were made of silk.

## Footwear

Romans wore leather sandals on their feet. In colder parts of the Empire socks were worn.

## Underwear

Underpants were worn by men, and women wore bikini-style underwear.

# Women's fashions

Girls and women wore long loose tunics and a dress called a **stola** which could be with or without sleeves. Stolae were always belted around the waist. Women's stolae went down to the ankles but girl's dresses stopped at the knees so that they could run about better. A shawl or hooded cloak could be worn on top for extra warmth.

Jewellery was very popular for both women and men. Lots of examples of earrings, necklaces, and bracelets have been dug up by archaeologists.

# Hairdressing

Blond hair was much admired by the Romans and at one time it was fashionable for ladies to wear yellow wigs or dye their hair yellow. Blonde hair had to be imported from Germany to make the blonde wigs. Curling tongs were used to curl both men and women's hair. Hairdressers also used pins and combs to create fancy hairstyles.

Children wore a **bulla**, a lucky charm, around their necks. A rich child might have a gold one but a poor child might only have one made of leather.

## Did you know?

The Romans collected urine in jars to use as washing detergent! It was used to bleach clothes white.

People taking part in government elections had their togas whitened by having pipe clay rubbed on. They were called **candidati** which meant 'whitened men'. Nowadays we still call people standing for elections 'candidates'.

# Roman food and feasting

A Roman's experience of food would very much depend on whether he or she was rich or poor. Bread, eggs, fruit (especially grapes), and vegetables were common to all. People near the sea would have plenty of fish to eat, whereas people in the country would depend on chicken, duck, rabbit, and other animals as meat sources. Wealthier people ate more meat and could afford to hold dinner parties.

## Evening meals

Most ordinary townspeople would wait until the evening to eat a proper meal. People living in crowded flats were not allowed fires for cooking in their homes, so they went out to get their hot food from Roman snack bars. They could buy stews, pies, or sausages to eat and diluted wine to drink, perhaps flavoured with spices and sweetened with honey. There were no sugar or chocolate treats as we have now. A form of pizza would have been enjoyed, but there were no tomatoes available in Roman times. Some pastas were made, including macaroni and linguine.

There were no potatoes or bananas in those days, but other vegetables were commonly grown.

A mosaic of a Roman bread oven.

# Feasting for the wealthy

Wealthy Romans enjoyed three meals a day, prepared for them by slaves. Dinner was called **cena**.

The first course or **gustum** was usually cold and could include eggs, sardines, mushrooms, snails, or dormice.

The **primae mensae** or main course would have been mainly boiled or roasted meat such as poultry, fish, lobsters, or wild boar. Many dishes were eaten with a salty fish-gut sauce called **liquamen**.

The **secundae mensae** or dessert course might have included fruits, cakes, or dates in honey. All of this would be washed down with water, grape juice, or wine.

Dinner in the garden.

# A banquet for guests

The rich would hold extravagant banquets. Invited guests would take off their shoes and have their feet washed by slaves. They would wash their hands before using their fingers to eat with. They lay back on **triclinium**, three couches around a low table. They would tuck into an 'eat all you can' buffet which could include delicacies such as brains of ostrich, flamingo tongues, and horsemeat sausages. The chef would disguise one food as another, such as making chicken look like fish.

## Did you know?

When guests got too full they left the table and went to a next-door room to be sick. This made space for eating more.

To show how much they were enjoying the meal, guests burped loudly.

The host would put on entertainment for guests during dinner. There might be juggling, dancing, music, and maybe even a gladiator fight!

# Useful words

**AD** Used in dates to indicate the number of years after the birth of Jesus Christ.

**amphitheatre** A large, semi-circular open area with sloping sides covered with rows of seats.

**aqueduct** A long bridge with many arches carrying a water supply over a valley

**arcade** A covered passage with shops or market stalls along one or both sides.

**archaeologist** Someone who studies the past by digging up and examining the remains of building, tools, or other things.

**atrium** The main hall of a Roman house with the central part of the roof open to the air.

**auxiliary** A person employed to help other members of staff.

**barbaric** Cruel or brutal.

**BC** Used in dates to indicate the number of years before the birth of Jesus Christ.

**bleach** When a material is turned white, usually by using a chemical.

**centurion** An ancient Roman officer in charge of around a hundred soldiers

**civilised** Having a developed social organisation and way of life

**cohort** An ancient Roman military unit, made up of six centuries, equal to one tenth of a legion

**colonnade** A row of evenly spaced columns supporting a roof or arches.

**concrete** A solid building material made by mixing cement, sand and water.

**conquer** When a person or an army takes control of another country by force.

**crossbow** A weapon consisting of a small bow fixed at the end of a piece of wood.

**detergent** A chemical substance for washing or cleaning things.

**dictator** A ruler who has complete power in a country, especially one who has taken power by force.

**empire** A group of countries under the rule of one state or person.

**foundation** A solid layer of concrete or bricks in the ground, on which a building is built to give it a firm base.

**founder** A person responsible for setting up an institution or organisation.

**freeman** A person who is not a slave.

**fresco** A picture painted on wet plaster on a wall.

**furnace** an enclosed chamber containing a very hot fire

**gladiator** Slaves trained to fight in arenas to provide entertainment in Ancient Rome. The word comes from Latin 'gladius' meaning sword.

**generation** The people of about the same age; also the period of time between one generation and the next, usually considered to be about 25 – 30 years.

**hearth** The floor of a fireplace.

**heir** The person who is entitled to inherit another person's property or a title.

**hippodrome** A stadium for chariot or horse races in ancient Greece or Rome.

**invade** When an army enters a country by force.

**invasion** The act of entering a country by force.

**legion** A military unit of between 3000 and 6000 soldiers in Ancient Rome.

**legionaire** The commander of a legion.

**lime** A chemical substance that is used in cement and as a fertiliser.

**myth** An untrue belief or explanation or a story which was made up long ago to explain natural events and religious beliefs.

**philosophy** The study or creation of ideas about existence, knowledge or beliefs.

**plague** A very infectious disease that kills large numbers of people.

**politician** A person involved in the government of a country.

**pozzolana** A volcanic material which makes concrete more resistant to salt water than modern-day concrete.

**proverb** A short sentence which gives advice or makes a comment about life.

**rampart** Banks of earth, often with a wall on top, that are built to protect a castle or city.

**republic** A country that has a president rather than a king or queen.

**settlement** A place where people have settled and built homes.

**shrine** A place of worship associated with a sacred person or object.

**stake** A pointed wooden post that can be hammered into the ground and used as a support.

**standard** A military or ceremonial flag carried on a pole.

**stylus** An ancient pen-like writing implement, with a pointed end for scratching letters on wax-covered tablets, and a blunt end for obliterating them.

**surrender** When a person or an army stops fighting and agrees that the other side has won.

**tactics** The ways in which troops and equipment are used in order to win a battle.

**temple** A building for worship.

**tier** One of a number of rows or layers of something.

**tragedy** A serious story or play, that usually ends with the death of the main character.

**turret** A small narrow tower on top of a larger tower or other buildings.

**tutor** A private teacher.

**unrest** Anger and dissatisfaction amongst the people of a city or country.

# Index

# Acknowledgements

**Publisher:** Anne Mahon
**Project Managers:** Craig Balfour, Robin Scrimgeour
**Designer:** Kevin Robbins
**Layout:** Robin Scrimgeour, Gordon MacGilp
**Index:** Lisa Footit
**Text:** Sarah Thurlbeck
**Editorial:** Maree Airlie

## Photo credits

Cover image
Statue of Caesar: Kevin H Knuth/Shutterstock.com
Map: Tom Grundy/Shutterstock.com
Ruins: alessandro0770/Shutterstock.com

t=top, c=centre, b=bottom, l=left, r=right
SS=Shutterstock

pp2-3, 22-23, 68-72 Radiocat/SS; pp4-5 Ahmad A Atwah/SS; pp6-7 © The Art Archive / Alamy Stock Photo; pp8-9 Robert Brown Stock/SS; p8 Andrei Nekrassov/SS (t), Jouve (b); p9 Paul Cowan/SS (t), Lefteris Papaulakis/SS (b); pp10-11 ecco/SS; p10 Kizel Cotiw-an/SS (t), Elena Dijour/SS (b); p11 Kevin H Knuth/SS (t), Malchev/SS (c), Malchev/SS (b); pp12-13 © PRISMA ARCHIVO / Alamy Stock Photo; pp14-15 wjarek/SS; p14 LevT/SS (t), Jouve (b); pp16-17 Radu Bercan/SS; p17 Jouve (t), meunierd/SS (b); pp18-19 eFesenko/SS; p18 Michael Rosskothen/SS; p18, p19, p22, p29 Peter Hermes Furian/SS; p19 © The Art Archive / Alamy Stock Photo; pp20-21 Pavel Ganchev - Paf/SS; p20 Shaun Jeffers/SS (t), Voropaev Vasiliy/SS (b); p21 tomy/SS (tr), Kiev.Victor/SS (tc), Lefteris Papaulakis/SS (tl), John Swope/Getty Images (b); p23 mishabender/SS (t), © North Wind Picture Archives / Alamy Stock Photo (c), Asier Villafranca/SS (b); pp24-25 Elias H. Debbas II/SS; p24 Cromagnon/SS (t), Kizel Cotiw-an/SS (b); p25 tristan tan/SS (tr), Sergey Kohl/SS (tl), yahiyat/SS (c), YuryZap/SS (b); pp26-27 pasdig79/SS; p26 Paul J Martin/SS (t), Giakita/SS (b); p27 Patricia Hofmeester/SS (t), Claudio Divizia/SS (c), Justin Black/SS (b); pp28-29 Dmitriy Krasko/SS; p28 Cris Foto/ SS (t), salajean/SS (b); p29 gunerkaya/ SS; pp30-31 Vladimir Korostyshevskiy/SS; p32 Deatonphotos/SS (t), SueC/SS (b); p33 3drenderings/SS (t), (c), A S E F/SS (bl), Regien Paassen/SS (br); pp34-35 Nejron Photo/SS; p34 Algol/SS; p35 Santi0103/SS; pp36-37 Dn Br/SS; p36 Kirill Nosov/SS; p37 Cortyn/SS (t), Jaime Pharr/SS (c); pp38-39 joeborg/SS; p40 Everett Collection/SS (t), lapas77/SS (b); p41 © Ivy Close Images / Alamy Stock Photo (t), Regien Paassen/SS (tr), Fernando Cortes/SS (c), Panos Karas/SS (b); p42 Fotokvadrat/SS; p43 Juan Aunion/SS (t), Logan81/SS (c), Feliks Kogan/SS (b); pp44-45 thefuzzball/SS; p44 © National Geographic Creative / Alamy Stock Photo (t), © National Geographic Creative / Alamy Stock Photo (b); p45 f8grapher/SS (t), ariadna de raadt/SS (c), mountainpix/SS (b); pp46-47 Wata51/SS; p46 Alexander A. Sobolev/SS (t), Tomacco/SS (c), Route66/SS (b); p47 Claudio Divizia/SS (t), mountainpix/SS (c), Christian Bertrand/SS (b); pp48-49 OZMedia/SS; p50 pavel dudek/SS (t), Jouve (b); p51 Khirman Vladimir/SS (t), Morphart Creation/SS (c), Nicola Galiero/SS (b); pp52-53 Sergio Foto/SS; p52 Porojnicu Stelian/SS (t), javarman/SS (b); p53 Porojnicu Stelian/SS (tr), khd/SS (tl), sharptoyou/SS (c), vlas2000/SS (b); p54 Viacheslav Lopatin/SS; p55 Jouve (t), Frank Bach/SS (c), Igor Polyakov/SS (b); pp56-57 Fabio Lamanna/SS; p56 Reidl/SS (t), anshar/SS (b); p57 Lukiyanova Natalia / frenta/SS (t), Aaron Wood/SS (cl), bopra77/SS (cr), Rainer Lesniewski/SS (bl), Gigi Peis/SS (br); p58-59 Bokstaz/SS; p58 Elena Elisseeva/SS (t), Gaby Fitz/SS; p59 Jannis Tobias Werner/SS (t), LianeM/SS (c), Emi Cristea/SS (b); pp60-61 © Lebrecht Music and Arts Photo Library / Alamy Stock Photo; pp62-63 James Steidl/SS; p62 Jouve (t), Victoria Gripas/SS (c), Thoom/SS (b); p63 Xseon/SS (t), A-R-T/SS (cl), Jouve (cr), Niakris6/SS (bl), © INTERFOTO / Alamy Stock Photo (br); pp64-65 Naypong/SS; p64 padu_foto/SS (tl), nikolay100/SS (tr), Jouve (b); p65 Jouve (t), Print Collector/Getty Images (c), ArtMari/SS (b); pp66-67 Shulevskyy Volodymyr/SS; p66 © Tim Gainey / Alamy Stock Photo (t), De Agostini/Archivio J. Lange/Getty Images (bl), © The Art Archive / Alamy Stock Photo (br); p67 © Lebrecht Music and Arts Photo Library / Alamy Stock Photo (t), © National Geographic Creative / Alamy Stock Photo (c), David Fowler/SS (b)

**Thanks to:**
Catherine Conn and Fiona Kerr